kawaii KRYPT

HAPPY
FUCKING
COLORING!

FUCK
TRUMPET

CHOOE
CHEDDAR

Fanny
FLAPS

SAUSAGE
STUFFER

TWAT
Rocket

FUCK
nugget

thunder
CUNT

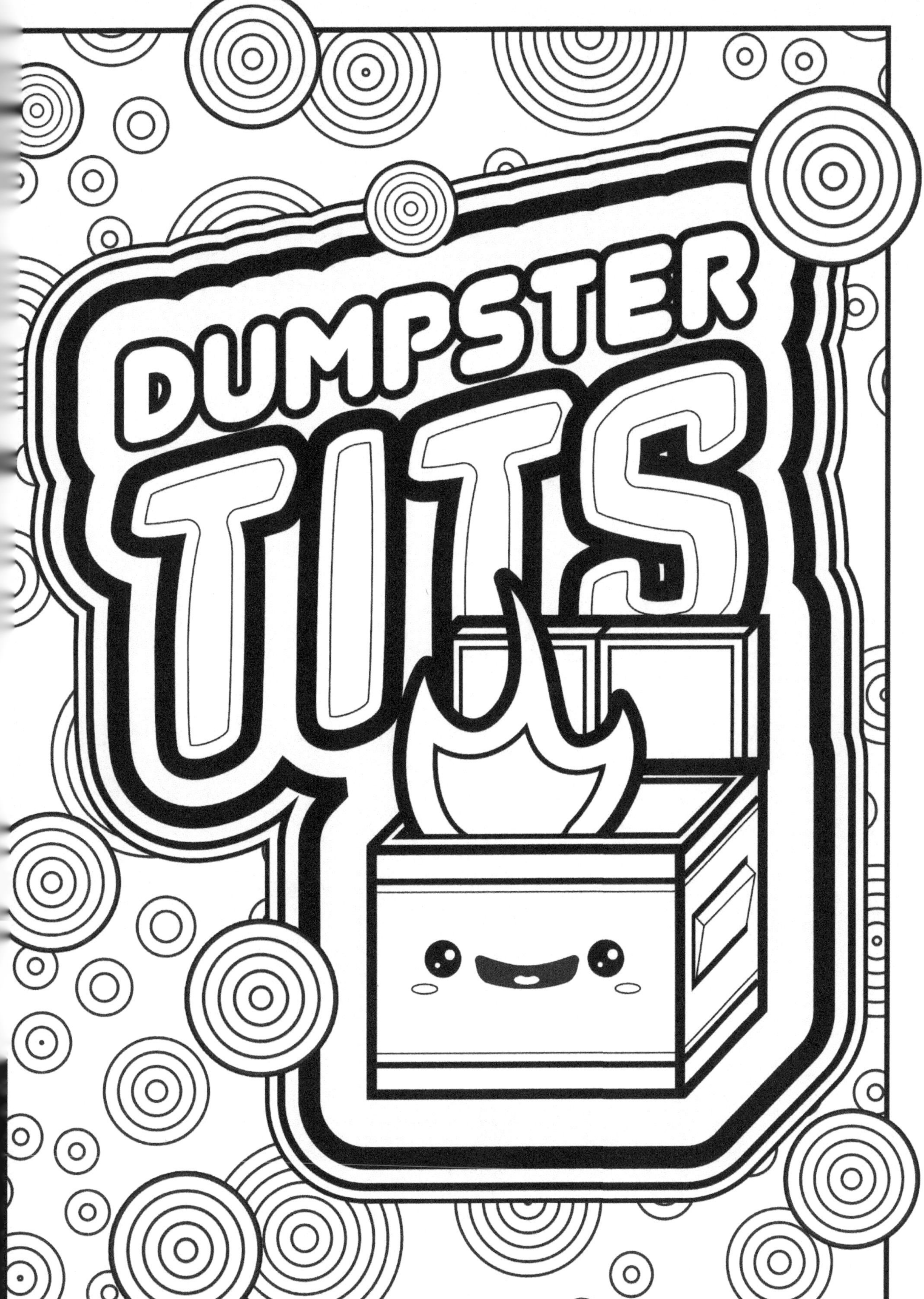
DUMPSTER
TITS

TARTER
TOSSER

BUTT
butter

dick
sauce

SCROTE
Snack

BEEF
BOOBS
MILK

JIZZ
MUFFIN.

Sweaty
SAX

TWAT
WAFFLE

KNOB
Cheese

COCK
BURGER

Pecker
HEAD

BLART

SCUM
SLURPER

CACK
SALAD

JIZZ
JOCKEY

KNOB
SHLOBBER

DICK
PICKLE

DOUCHE
CANOE

PRICK
LICKER

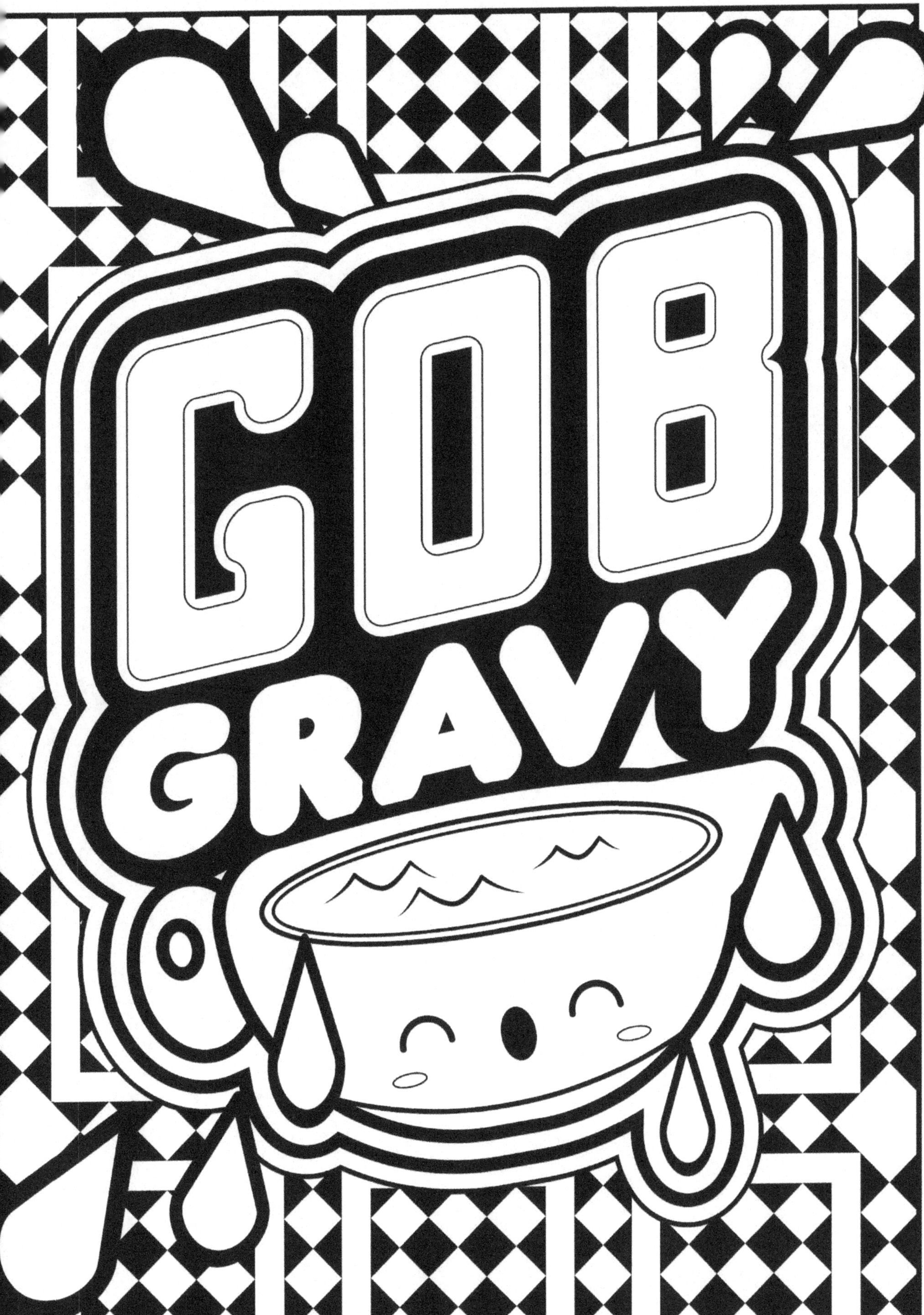
GOB
GRAVY

HAM
HOLE

SALAD
SNIFFER

Made in the USA
Las Vegas, NV
06 December 2023

82205385R00037